IF YOU WERE A . . .

Ballplayer

IF YOU WERE A . . .
Ballplayer

Virginia Schomp

BENCHMARK BOOKS

MARSHALL CAVENDISH
NEW YORK

Baseball and basketball are games of high-flying excitement.

If you were a ballplayer, you'd step up to home plate. You'd swing your bat—*whack!* That baseball's a missile headed out of the park.

Will you play basketball? You'll need quick hands and high-flying feet.

In soccer and football, players race for the goal.

Soccer? Get ready to think fast and run hard. Football? Maybe you'll grab a pass and score a touchdown to help your team win the Super Bowl.

Excitement and fun and lots of hard work—they'd all be part of the game, if you were a ballplayer.

At training camp, pitcher Randy Johnson works on his ninety-five-mile-an-hour fastball.

It's February. In many places, the ground is covered with snow. But at training camps in Florida and Arizona, it feels like spring—and that means it's time for baseball.

Spring training gives ballplayers a chance to get in shape for the coming season. Hitters practice batting. Pitchers toss ball after ball. During practice games, the players sharpen their baserunning, fielding, and other skills. Through hard work, they learn to play together as a team.

Spring-training workouts stretch and strengthen ballplayers' muscles.

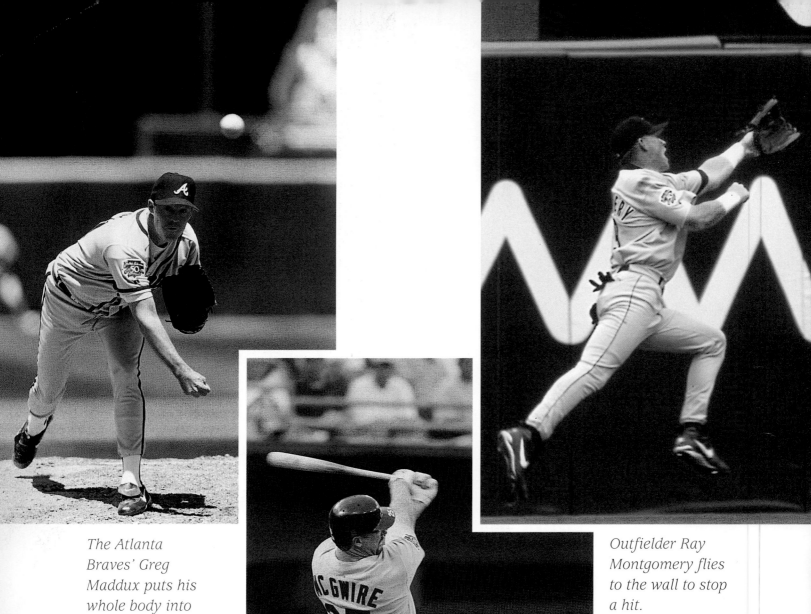

The Atlanta
Braves' Greg
Maddux puts his
whole body into
the pitch.

Outfielder Ray
Montgomery flies
to the wall to stop
a hit.

In 1998 slugger
Mark McGwire
made baseball
history by hitting
a record seventy
home runs.

A split second can make the difference between "safe" and "out."

"Play ball!" the umpire hollers. It's opening day of baseball season. Fans cheer as their favorite players take the field.

If you were a batter, you might slam a line drive to the outfield wall. Running hard, you make it to second base. Next batter—a solid hit. You round third and head for home. The ball flies toward the catcher's mitt. You slide into the plate. Safe!

Major league baseball teams are divided into the American and National Leagues. Each league has three divisions—Eastern, Western, and Central.

In September the best teams from each division face each other in the League Championship Series. Then the American and National League champions battle it out in the World Series. The first team to win four games becomes the champion of the baseball world.

The San Francisco Giants pile it on after winning the National League's 1997 Western Division play-offs.

Basketball superstar Michael Jordan won his fifth NBA Finals Most Valuable Player Award in 1997.

The champion of men's professional basketball is the team that wins the National Basketball Association play-offs. The NBA is divided into two conferences—the Eastern and Western. Millions of fans watch on TV as the leaders of the Eastern and Western Conferences compete for the championship crown.

Basketball is a fast-moving sport. If you played for the NBA, you might run three miles in one forty-eight-minute game. The ball is a blur as you dribble it past a defender. Will you pass? Or charge the basket for a soaring slam dunk?

Michael Jordan shows the slam-bang style that helped the Chicago Bulls win the 1997 NBA championship.

Teresa Edwards glides past a defender in the 1998 women's pro basketball All-Star Game.

Fans of women's basketball don't see many dunk shots. Players in the Women's National Basketball Association aren't as tall as most NBA stars. But some fans say the players work harder on skills like dribbling and faking passes. And that makes WNBA games even more exciting.

The Houston Comets lost this game but went on to win the 1997 championship.

The U.S.A. and Iran battle for the ball in the 1998 World Cup play-offs.

Dribbling and passing are important skills in soccer, too. But in this sport, players make their moves with feet instead of hands.

If you were a soccer goalie, you would watch your teammates race up the field. Their quick feet tap and kick the ball toward the opposite goal. Suddenly the other team gets the ball. A wall of players thunders toward you. You dive through the air to grab the ball and keep the attackers from scoring.

A diving save stops a goal. Goalies are the only players allowed to touch the ball with their hands.

The French team celebrates winning World Cup 1998.

The U.S.A. and New Zealand compete for the right to play in the 1999 Women's World Cup.

Powerful goal shots and diving saves make soccer exciting to play and to watch. All that excitement has made soccer the most popular sport in the world.

More than one billion fans watch the World Cup tournament in person and on TV. The World Cup is held every four years. Soccer teams from twenty-four different countries compete. In 1998 France clobbered defending champion Brazil in the final match.

Green Bay Packers quarterback Brett Favre gets set to let the ball fly.

In most of the world, the sport we call soccer is known as football. But in the United States and Canada, football is a separate game packed with power and thrills.

Imagine two speedy trains meeting head-on. That's what it's like at the start of a football game. One team kicks off. The other catches the ball and runs it back up the field, toward the goal. The kicking team's players race toward the ballcarrier. The two teams meet. Bodies slam. Ouch!

Football is a game of action and hard hits.

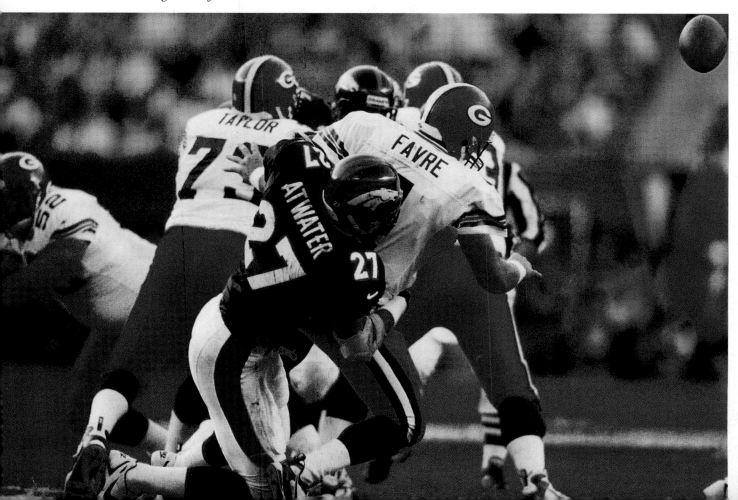

Running backs need speed.

Receivers need good hands and great moves.

Each player on the football team has a special job. Running backs run with the ball. Wide receivers catch passes. Defensive linemen try to tackle the quarterback before he can pass.

If you were a quarterback, you'd lead the offense when your team has the ball. You would call the signals and take the ball at the start of each play. You might hand it off to a running back or throw a pass to a receiver. You might scramble to score the winning touchdown.

The quarterback's mission is to protect the ball and move it toward the goal.

Touchdown! Home run! Slam dunk! Goal! Whether you played football or baseball, basketball or soccer, you would always keep one eye on the score. Your mission—to win the game. And the next game, and the next. Your dream—to lead your team all the way to the championship.

Super Bowl XXXII celebration—Denver welcomes home its championship football team, the Broncos.

Young ballplayers learn to stay alert and ready for action.

Every sport calls for different talents and training. But all ballplayers start with a love of their game. Most professional players began

Practice helps future sports stars sharpen their skills.

their careers as part of a school or community team. They worked hard to learn the rules, stay fit, and improve their skills.

Wearing the right gear helps prevent injuries.

It's not easy to become a pro ballplayer. Only the very best players make it to the top. But if you have the talent and the hunger to succeed, you might join the lucky athletes who play ball.

Most important of all, playing sports is fun!

BALLPLAYERS IN TIME

Early British colonists brought stick-and-ball games to America. By the 1800s, "Base Ball" was the country's number-one game.

The first U.S. women's professional baseball league played during World War II. It entertained Americans while many of the men of the major leagues fought in the war.

In 1947 Jackie Robinson became the first black ballplayer to play in the major leagues.

The great Wilt Chamberlain once scored one hundred points in a single basketball game.

Many fans have called Pelé the best soccer player of all time.

Early football players did not wear uniforms or helmets. Many were badly injured or killed.

This book is for Leor,
who can hit to all fields and touch every base

Benchmark Books
Marshall Cavendish Corporation
99 White Plains Road
Tarrytown, New York 10591
Copyright © 2000 by Marshall Cavendish Corporation

Library of Congress Cataloging-in-Publication Data
Schomp, Virginia, date.
If you were a—ballplayer / Virginia Schomp.   p.   cm.
Summary: Introduces the skills, equipment and training that are part of competition in the sports
of baseball, basketball, soccer, and football.
!SBN 0-7614-0917-3
1. Ball games—Juvenile literature. [1. Ball games. 2. Athletes.] I. Title.
GV861.S35 1999   796.3—dc21   99-12651   CIP

Photo research by Rose Corbett Gordon

Cover: *Allsport USA:* Otto Greule; Doug Pensinger (top insert); Zoran Milich
(center insert); Jamie Squire (bottom insert)

Mark Needleman: 1, 31. *Allsport USA:*29 (top right); Rick Stewart, 4 (left), 23; Jonathan Daniel, 4 (right), 13, 30 (bottom left); David Leah, 5 (left); Andy Lyons, 5 (right), 8 (bottom center), 14; Brian Bahr, 6, 12, 22 (right); Jeff Carlick, 7; Todd Warshaw, 8 (top left), 15, 30 (top right); Harry How, 8 (top right); Al Bello, 9 (right), 20, 21; Otto Greule, 10-11, 30 (bottom right); Vandystadt, 16; Aubrey Washington, 18 (left); Stu Forster, 19; Scott Halleran, 22 (left); Nevin Reid, 24-25; Mike Powell, 27 (right); Kirk Schlea, 30 (top left). *The Image Bank/Yellow Dog Productions:*17. *Index Stock Imagery:*Frank Siteman, 26 (left), 27 (left); Dennis MacDonald, 26 (right). *North Wind Picture Archives:*28 (top left). *UPI/Corbis-Bettmann:*28 (right). *Archive Photos:*28 (bottom left), 29 (top and bottom left).

Printed in Hong Kong
1   3   5   7   8   6   4   2

INDEX